What's Cooking?

A fun guide to food science, healthy eating and recipes
from around the world

Gabrielle Woolfitt

*With photography by APM
Photographic*

Wayland

What's Cooking?

*A fun guide to food science, healthy eating and
recipes from around the world*

Notes for Teachers

This book is designed for use at Key Stage 2 although the content is suitable for older
children too. *What's Cooking?* is relevant to the Technology Curriculum. It is also relevant to
the Science Curriculum: AT 1 (Scientific Investigation), AT 2 (Life and Living Processes),
and AT 3 (Materials and their Properties).

Editor: Cath Senker
Designer: Jean Wheeler
Studio photography by APM Photographic
Photo stylist: Zoë Hargreaves
Production controller: Carol Stevens
Cover design: Loraine Hayes
Cover illustration: Jackie Harland

First published in 1994 by Wayland (Publishers) Ltd
61 Western Road, Hove, East Sussex, BN3 1JD, England

British Library Cataloguing in Publication Data
Woolfitt, Gabrielle
What's Cooking?
I. Title
641.3

ISBN 0-7502-0984-4

Typeset by Jean Wheeler
Printed and bound by G. Canale C.S.p.A., Turin, Italy

Contents

What's cooking?

**Cooking is all about making food ready to eat.
This book will help you to cook some delicious food.
It also tells you how to keep food fresh. Here is some
advice to read before you start:**

1 Good cooks keep everything in the kitchen clean. This is called food hygiene. Always wash your hands before you start to cook. Wash your hands again after preparing raw food.

These children have cleaned the kitchen before they start to cook.

● Put on an apron for cooking and tie back your hair if it is long.

● Always use clean cloths and tea towels.

● Wash all the utensils in hot, soapy water after you have used them, and then rinse off the soap.

2 Cook safely. In this book you will sometimes see a triangle sign,  which means you need to take special care. You should always ask an older person to help you when you see the triangle.

These things in the kitchen can be dangerous:

- sharp knives
- a hot oven
- heavy saucepans
- a grater
- mess on the floor.

3 Follow the recipe. Read it through before you start and make sure you have everything you need.

There will be a list of the ingredients and then a list of the utensils. They are written in the order in which you will use them.

All the recipes in this book are safe if you follow the instructions.

Even if you cook every day, it still takes years to learn to be a good cook. If you start to practise now you could be a top chef when you are older!

A balanced diet

We all need a balanced diet. This means we should eat lots of different types of food. If you eat a balanced diet, you should be fit and healthy. You need the right kinds of food as well as the right amount.

This pyramid is one way to show the different food groups. It shows you how much of each type of food you should eat every day.

Group 4 (Milk, yoghurt and cheese) **2–3 servings** These foods are very important for growing children. They contain lots of calcium and protein. Calcium is needed for your bones and teeth to grow strong. Milk has Vitamin B, which helps the brain to work properly.

Group 2 (Vegetables) **3–5 servings** Different vegetables give you different vitamins. Vitamins are special chemicals that are found in some foods. Small amounts of vitamins are needed for the body to work. Vitamin A comes from carrots, most dark green vegetables and from some fruit. It helps your eyesight.

Group 1 (Bread, cereal, rice and pasta) **6–11 servings** These foods give you energy. Wholemeal bread and bran cereals have lots of fibre. Fibre helps food to move down through your body.

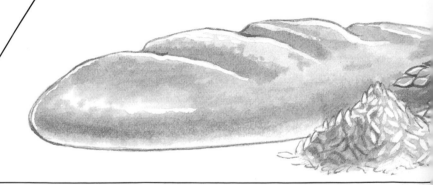

Group 6 (Fats, oils and sugar)
Foods such as crisps,
chocolate, biscuits and
cakes. You should try to
eat as little of these
foods as possible.
They can make
you fat and rot
your teeth.

Write down everything you eat in one day. Work out which groups all the foods fit into. Check if you are eating a balanced diet by counting how many servings you ate from each food group.

Group 5 (Meat, poultry, fish, eggs and pulses) **2–3 servings** Protein from
these foods keeps your body strong
and helps it to grow. Most of
your body is made of protein,
even your hair. Eggs have
Vitamin D, which keeps
bones and teeth healthy.

Group 3 (Fruit) **2–4 servings**
Fruit contains vitamins.
Vitamin C is found in
oranges and strawberries.
It helps the body to fight
germs.

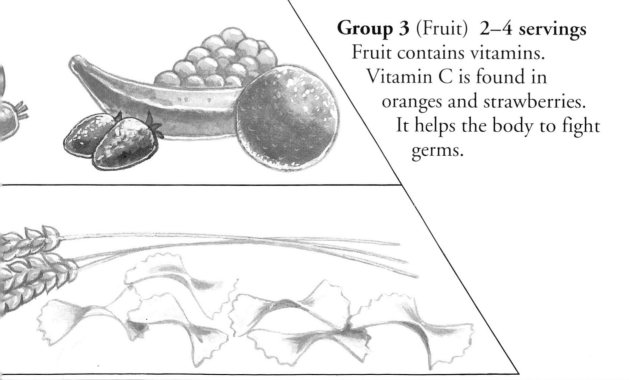

Why food goes off

Sometimes milk tastes and smells strange. This means that it has 'gone off'. All food will go off if it is kept in the wrong way.

This experiment is about what makes milk go off. Choose a warm morning to try it. The temperature should be about 15-20° Celsius (C).

You will need:
- 500 ml of fresh milk
- four cups
- measuring jug
- bowl

1 Measure 125 ml of milk into each cup using a measuring jug.

2 Put the first cup of milk into the fridge.

3 Put the second cup of milk on a table in a cool room.

4 Put the third cup of milk on a sunny windowsill where it will become warm.

5 Gently lower the last cup of milk into a bowl of very warm water. Leave it until the water has cooled down. Then put it next to the other cup on the windowsill.

6 After three hours, smell all the cups of milk. DO NOT TASTE THEM. Write down where each cup of milk was and how it smelt. Then put all the cups back and leave them for another few hours.

7 At the end of the day, smell all the cups again. Which cup of milk still smells fresh? Which cup of milk smells the worst? Now pour all the milk away and wash the cups.

Can you see a pattern that tells you what made the milk go off? Now you know why we keep milk in the fridge.

Microbes and food

There are microbes in all fresh food. They are so small that you need a microscope to see them. There are good microbes and bad microbes. There are good ones that help to turn milk into cheese or yoghurt. The bad ones can make you very ill. If food smells bad it usually means that it has got too many bad microbes in it. You should never eat food that has gone bad.

All people are covered in microbes. But it is important not to let bad microbes get into your food. This is why you must always wash and dry your hands before you start cooking.

A microbe can split into two new ones every twenty minutes, if it is warm. So if you have just one microbe on a piece of food there could be two after twenty minutes, four after forty minutes and eight after an hour.

How many will there be after two hours? After seven hours there would be over two million microbes. You can see why we must keep food cool!

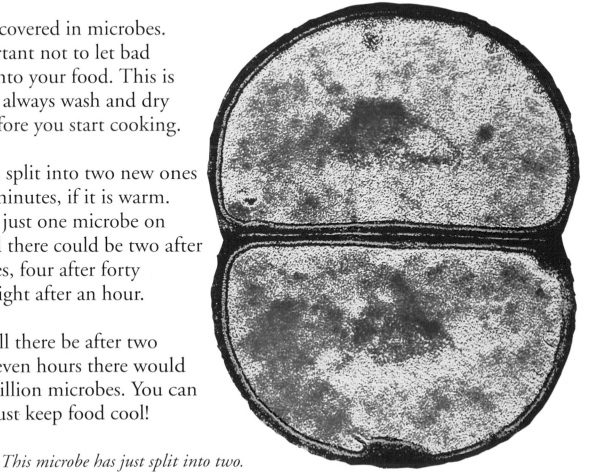

This microbe has just split into two.

10

Yeast is a good kind of microbe. When yeast is put into warm water with some sugar, it starts to go frothy. Yeast cells turn sugar into alcohol and bubbles of carbon dioxide gas. Yeast is used to make bread. The bubbles inside a loaf of bread are made of the gas that the yeast makes.

Above *Here, yeast has been added to warm water.*

Left *A baker kneading and shaping dough.*

On the next page there is a recipe for making bread. You will use yeast. You will also knead the dough. This does two things. It spreads the yeast around the dough. This means that the bubbles are made all the way through the dough. The kneading also stretches out the flour. This makes the dough stronger, so the bread will keep the shape of the bubbles better.

Making bread

Here is a simple recipe for making bread.

You will need:
- some vegetable oil
- 370 g of strong bread flour (wholemeal is best)
- 1 teaspoon of salt
- 1 tablespoon of solid vegetable fat
- 1/2 sachet of fast-acting dried yeast (if you use a different kind of yeast you must follow the instructions on the packet)
- 225 ml of warm water
- some flour for kneading
- 500 g loaf tin
- big mixing bowl
- sharp knife
- large spoon for mixing
- large breadboard
- large piece of microwave-quality clingfilm
- blunt knife
- wire rack

1 Rub the oil all over the inside of the loaf tin. Then sift the flour into the bowl. Add the salt.

2 Cut the fat into small pieces with the sharp knife. Rub the fat into the flour until it is all mixed in (see right).

3 Mix in the dried yeast. Pour in the warm water and stir the mixture. Use your hands to form it into a lump of dough.

4 Sprinkle a little flour on to the breadboard. Take the dough out of the bowl and put it on to the board.

5 Knead the dough for ten minutes. You need to stretch it out with your knuckles and then fold it back together again.

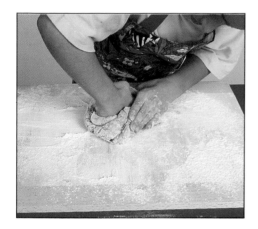

6 When the dough is soft and stretchy, put it into the loaf tin. Put a little oil on to the clingfilm and cover the bread with the oiled side.

7 Put the dough in a warm place to prove until the dough is twice as big as it was. Put the oven on at gas mark 6 (200° C or 400° Fahrenheit).

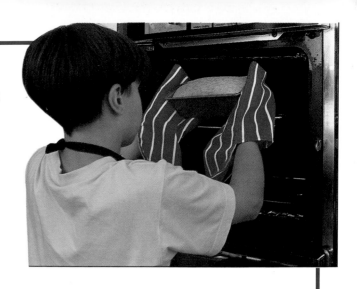

8 Take the clingfilm off the dough. Put your bread into the oven for thirty to forty minutes. Then take it out and let it cool in the tin for five minutes.

9 Take a blunt knife around the edge of the tin to loosen the bread. Carefully take the bread out of the tin and put it on to a wire rack until it is cool enough to eat.

Fresh bread smells and tastes delicious. Don't eat it all yourself!

Fresh food is healthy food

Microbes can make food go bad, so it is important to eat fresh food. If you grow some of your own food you will know that it is really fresh. You can grow cress in a few days.

You will need:

- cotton wool
- an empty margarine tub
- cress seeds
- water

1 Spread a thin layer of cotton wool on the bottom of the margarine tub.

2 Pour water on to the cotton wool so that it is quite wet.

3 Sprinkle cress seeds on to the cotton wool.

4 Leave the seeds in a sunny place for a few days. Keep the cotton wool damp.

When your cress has grown to the top of the tub it is ready to eat. You can make carrot, cress and cheese salad.

For two people you need:

- 1 large carrot
- 100 g of hard cheese
- fresh cress

- potato peeler
- grater
- bowl
- kitchen scissors
- large spoon for mixing
- salad bowl

1 Peel the carrot with the potato peeler.

2 Grate the carrot and the cheese into a bowl. Be careful not to grate your fingers. ⚠️

3 Take the cress, with the cotton wool, out of the tub. Rinse it in water for a couple of seconds.

4 Snip the cress off the cotton wool with the scissors and put it into the bowl with the cheese and the carrot.

5 Mix everything together.

6 Serve your salad in a pretty bowl with bread for lunch. You can also use cress in sandwiches.

Making tzatziki

Here is another simple, fresh dish. Tzatziki is easy to make and tastes delicious. It is a traditional Greek first course. You can eat it with pitta bread as a quick snack, with crisps as a dip, or with a main course as a salad.

To make enough for four people you will need:

- half a cucumber
- two sprigs of fresh mint (or dried mint)
- small pot of plain yoghurt (Greek yoghurt is best)
- pinch of salt
- one or two cloves of garlic (if you like it)

- potato peeler
- knife
- colander
- kitchen scissors
- small bowl
- salad bowl
- garlic press

1 Wash the cucumber in cold water.

2 Peel the skin off the cucumber using a potato peeler.

3 Cut the cucumber into small pieces. If you want to eat tzatziki as a dip, you need to cut the cucumber into very small pieces.

4 Put the cucumber pieces into a colander (above left) and leave them to drain for about twenty minutes.

5 Wash the fresh mint. Peel the leaves off the stem.

6 Snip the leaves into small pieces using kitchen scissors. Drop them into a small bowl.

7 Put the yoghurt into a salad bowl. Add the chopped mint (or dried mint) and a pinch of salt. Crush the garlic with the garlic press and add it too.

8 Add the cucumber and stir well. Now you can eat your tzatziki. It is best to eat this dish on the day you make it.

Pulses and making felafel

Pulses are foods such as chickpeas, kidney beans, lentils and haricot beans. Pulses are full of protein and they are usually very cheap.

Many dried pulses contain poisons. They must be soaked overnight in cold water. Then they are boiled for ten minutes until the poison has gone, and cooked until they are soft. The pulses you buy in a tin have already been soaked and cooked.

Felafel are spicy burgers made from chickpeas. They are eaten as a snack in Middle Eastern countries.

aduki beans — chickpeas

mung beans

lentils

kidney beans

haricot beans

To make about eight felafel you will need:

- 400 g tin of chickpeas
- 1 onion
- 1 pinch of salt and one of black pepper
- 1 teaspoon of cumin powder
- 1 clove of garlic
- flour for sprinkling
- 4 tablespoons of vegetable oil

- food processor or potato masher
- mixing bowl
- sharp knife
- garlic press
- large spoon for mixing
- chopping board
- frying pan
- slotted spoon
- kitchen roll

1 Put the chickpeas into the food processor and turn it on. Break up the chickpeas until they look like fine breadcrumbs. Scoop them into the bowl with the spoon. Or mash the chickpeas in the bowl with a potato masher.

6 An older person should fry the burgers in hot oil. When they are golden brown on one side (this will take about four minutes), turn them over to fry the other side.

2 Carefully chop up the onion into very small pieces using a knife or the food processor.

3 Put the onion into the bowl with the salt, pepper and cumin. Crush or chop the garlic and add that too. Mix everything together.

5 Take a small handful of the mixture and shape it into a small, flat burger. Put the burger on to the board and turn it over so that both sides have flour on. Make all the mixture into burgers.

7 When the felafel are cooked on both sides, carefully take them out of the pan with the slotted spoon. Put them on kitchen roll to drain off the oil.

8 Serve your felafel hot or cold, in pitta bread with salad. You can store felafel in the fridge for up to two days.

4 Wash and dry the chopping board. Then sprinkle it with flour.

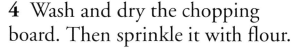

Check your diet

Some people have to watch what they eat because there are foods that make them ill. Other people are careful about what they eat because they believe it is wrong to eat certain foods.

If you get asthma, eczema or hay fever, you might be allergic to some foods. This means that you become ill if you eat them. Cows' milk, eggs and wheat are three foods that can cause allergies.

Below There are additives in fruit squash to make it bright orange.

Right This girl is sneezing because she has hay fever.

Above Different colourings are added to sweets.

Additives are chemicals that are added to food when it is produced in factories. Colours and flavours are often added to make food look or taste better. Some children become hyperactive if they have certain additives in their food. They find it hard to keep still and to sleep at night. One example is a yellow colouring that is sometimes used in orange squash. Hyperactive children must be careful about what they eat and drink.

Left Using a spinhaler can help to stop asthma.

If you have diabetes, your body does not use up sugar properly. A diabetic person must not eat too many sweet foods. Diabetics should try to eat foods with lots of fibre in them. Some need to have injections every day to keep them well. Others can stay well by eating exactly what their doctor tells them to.

Some people choose not to eat certain foods. Vegetarians don't eat any meat because they think it is wrong to kill animals. Vegans also don't eat eggs, milk or even honey, because they come from animals.

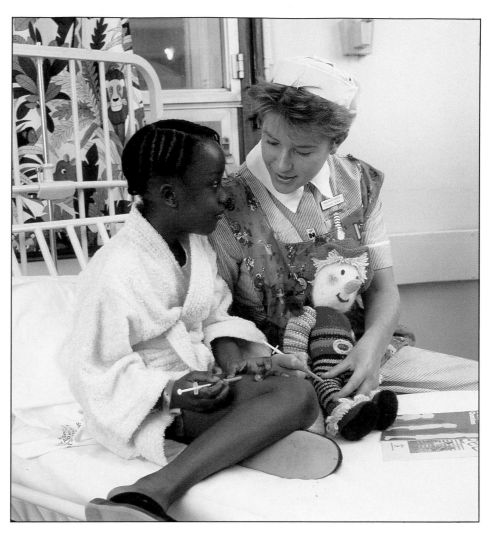

Above A nurse teaching a young diabetic girl how to inject herself with insulin.

Religious Jews and Muslims don't eat pork and other meat from a pig because they believe that pigs are not clean. Pork can make you ill if it is not properly prepared.

Before you invite friends for a meal, always ask if there are any foods which they do not eat.

Get the temperature right!

Some foods need to be cooked before we can eat them. The microbes in meat can make you ill if you don't cook the meat properly. Cooking kills the microbes.

Cooking also changes the feel and the taste of food. It makes a chemical change in the food. Bread dough is soft and squishy and it tastes bad, but cooked bread is firm and tastes good. Think of some foods that are hard, but become soft when they are cooked. Think of others which are cooked to get rid of poisons.

A cook making meringues. They will dry out slowly in a cool oven.

The food in this pan is simmering. The temperature is 100° C, or just below 100° C.

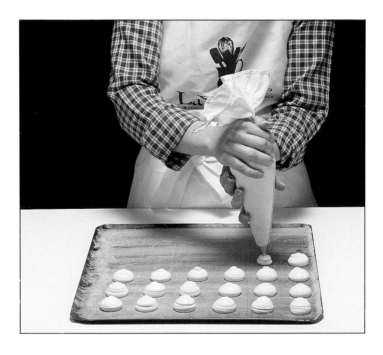

Modern cookers have a temperature control knob. You can decide how hot to cook your food.

Some food needs to be cooked very quickly at a high temperature. Chips fry in hot oil at 190° C. They only take three minutes to cook.

Meringues are cooked for several hours at only 70° C. Foods which are boiled in water are cooked at 100° C. If you are cooking with microbes, you have to keep them just warm, at around 37° C. They grow best at this temperature. It is our body temperature too.

Many different sweets can be made out of sugar. It all depends on how hot the sugar gets. Remember, you should only eat sweets as a special treat.

At 116° C you can make fudge. If the sugar gets just 4° C hotter it turns into chewy caramel.

If the sugar is not cooked at all, you can make peppermint creams.

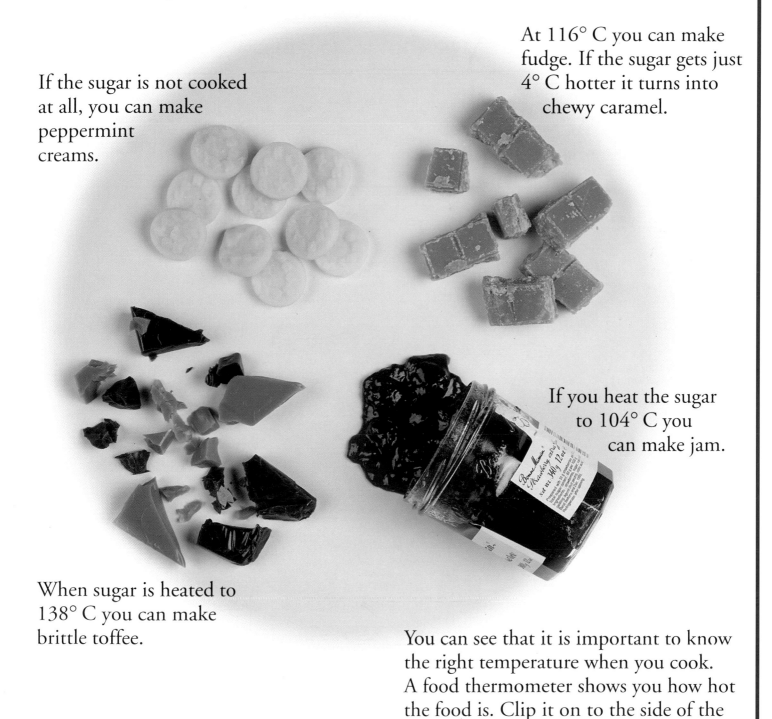

If you heat the sugar to 104° C you can make jam.

When sugar is heated to 138° C you can make brittle toffee.

You can see that it is important to know the right temperature when you cook. A food thermometer shows you how hot the food is. Clip it on to the side of the pan you are using.

Banana ice-cream

Some food needs to be really cold before it is ready to eat. On a hot day, ice-cream is a delicious way of cooling down. It is easy to make banana ice-cream.

To make enough for six people you will need:

- 1 lemon
- 250 ml of whipping cream
- 2 large, slightly soft bananas
- 40 g of soft brown sugar

- lemon squeezer
- electric whisk or hand whisk
- 2 mixing bowls
- fork
- large spoon
- ice-cream box with a lid

3 Mash the bananas with the sugar in the other bowl using the fork. Make sure there are no lumps.

1 Cut the lemon into halves and squeeze out all the juice, using the lemon squeezer.

2 Whisk the cream in a bowl until it makes peaks which stay. This will take 5–10 minutes with a hand whisk. (If you whisk the cream for too long, it will turn into butter in the end!)

4 Add the lemon juice.

5 Use the spoon to stir the cream into the banana mixture until it is smooth.

6 Put the mixture into the ice-cream box. Put the lid on and put it into the freezer to set.

7 After four hours the ice-cream will be frozen solid. Before you eat it, take it out of the freezer and leave it in the fridge for an hour. It will become softer and easier to serve.

If everyone loves your banana ice-cream you could try making frozen yoghurt. It is less fattening than ice-cream. Just use natural yoghurt instead of cream. Leave out the sugar from the recipe to make it even healthier. You could also try making other flavours of frozen yoghurt by using different fruits.

It looks good enough to eat

We all like food to taste and smell good. People also choose food because of the way it looks. If you make a brown-coloured stew and serve it with brown-skinned potatoes and soggy brown dumplings, it looks dull.

It is a good idea to put different-coloured foods together. A plate of bright vegetable salad, yellow sweetcorn and some roast chicken looks tasty because it is colourful.

Which of these two meals do you think looks more tasty?

You can do an experiment to find out which colours of food people prefer to eat.

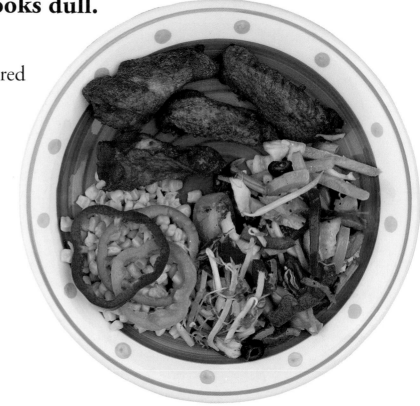

You will need:

- 200 g of icing sugar
- water
- food colouring in 3 different colours (such as red, yellow and blue)
- packet of plain biscuits
- 4 bowls, one larger than the others
- 4 spoons, one for stirring each of the four bowls of icing
- flat knife
- large plate

1 Put the icing sugar into the larger bowl. Add water one drop at a time. Stir the water into the icing sugar to make a thick paste.

2 Divide the icing between the four bowls.

4 Add two drops of red colouring to the second bowl of icing and two drops of blue colouring to the third bowl of icing. Use a different spoon for stirring each bowl of icing. Leave the last bowl of icing white.

5 Use the flat knife to spread icing sugar on to the biscuits. Use all the different colours. Spread the biscuits out on a large plate for the icing to set.

6 At tea-time offer the biscuits to your friends and see which colours they choose first. Which biscuits do they not want to eat?

3 Add two drops of yellow colouring to the first bowl of icing and stir it in.

Planning a meal

Planning a meal means more than just cooking.
At what time of day is the meal going to be? Who is
coming to the meal? How many people will there be?
Do any of them eat special food? These pictures show
Vicky planning a meal for herself and three friends.

It's **Wednesday**. Vicky wants to cook lunch on Saturday. One of her friends does not eat meat. She decides to make felafel, bread, tzatziki, and carrot, cheese and cress salad. For pudding they will have banana ice-cream.

Vicky looks up the recipes to find out which ingredients to buy and how much of each food she will need. She sees that some of the ingredients are already in the store cupboard. You could write her list by looking up the recipes in this book.

Vicky starts growing the cress right away.

Thursday Vicky goes shopping with her older brother. Then she makes the ice-cream. It will stay fresh in the freezer for a few days.

Saturday morning
Vicky makes the felafel. She prepares the tzatziki and the salad, and covers them with clingfilm. They will stay fresh in the fridge for a couple of hours. She takes the ice-cream out of the fridge an hour before lunch.

Friday Vicky bakes the bread. She stores it in a plastic bag in the food cupboard.

What else must Vicky remember to do?

Glossary

Celsius (C) scale A temperature scale. Ice melts at 0° C, and water boils at 100° C.

Chef A cook, usually the main cook.

Colander A pan with holes in the bottom, used for rinsing and draining food.

Diet The foods that you eat every day make up your diet.

Dough A thick mixture of flour and water, used for making bread.

Fat The greasy part of food that gives you energy to store in your body. You should only eat a little fat.

Felafel Spicy chickpea burgers eaten as a snack in the Middle East.

Fibre The part of food that helps you to digest what you eat.

Food hygiene Keeping everything clean when you work with food.

Ingredients The foods that are needed for a recipe.

Knead To stretch bread dough so that the yeast can start to work.

Oils Fats that are runny. They are usually made from plants.

Protein The part of food that helps you to grow.

Prove To leave dough to rise in a warm place before you bake it.

Pulses Dried peas or beans. They usually need to be soaked and boiled before they can be eaten.

Recipe A list of ingredients and instructions for making a food dish.

Set To become solid.

Temperature The measure of how hot or cold something is.

Thermometer An instrument used to measure temperature.

Utensils The tools that are used for cooking.

Vegans People who do not eat any foods which come from animals.

Vegetarians People who do not eat meat or fish, or foods with meat or fish in them.

Vitamins Special chemicals that are found in some foods. Small amounts of vitamins are needed for the body to work.

Finding out more

Burgers and Bugs: The Science Behind Food by Lesley Newson (Piccolo, 1991)

Diet by Brian Ward (Franklin Watts, 1991)

Diet and Health by Ida Weekes (Wayland, 1991)

E for Additives by Maurice Hanssen (Thorsons, 1987)

Fast Food Cook Book by Susannah Bradley (Henderson Publishing, 1991)

Food and Diet (Heinemann Children's Reference, 1990)

Food Facts series: *Fats* by Rhoda Nottridge; *Fibre* by Jane Inglis; *Proteins* by Jane Inglis; *Sugar* by Rhoda Nottridge; *Vitamins* by Rhoda Nottridge (all Wayland 1992)

Food for Thought by Gill Standing (A&C Black, 1990)

Food Fun Book by Rosemary Stanton (Hamlyn, 1988)

Food Hygiene by Pete Sanders (Franklin Watts, 1990)

Healthy Eating by Wayne Jackman (Wayland, 1990)

Healthy Food by James Erlichman (Franklin Watts, 1990)

Keep out of the Kitchen, Mum by Jill Cox (Deutsch, 1991)

The Sainsbury Book of Children's Cookery by Roz Denny and Caroline Waldegrave (J Sainsbury plc, 1993)

Scrumptious Veggie Cook Book: for Kids and Others by Marianne Bird (Green Print, 1991)

Soul Cakes and Shish Kebabs: Multifaith Cookery Book (Religious and Moral Education Publishing, 1987)

Acknowledgements
The publishers would like to thank the following for permission to reproduce photographs in this book: Cephas Picture Library 11 (below); Chapel Studios (Z Mukhida) *cover*, 5, 11 (above); Eye Ubiquitous (Y Nikiteas) 20 (second from left), (P Seheult) 20 (far right), (A Beszant) 22 (below); Greg Evans International Photo Library (G B Evans) 20 (second from right), (G B Evans) 21 (below); Science Photo Library (Dr T Brain) 10, (J Durham) 20 (bottom), (St Bartholomew's Hospital) 21 (above); Topham 22 (above); Wayland (Z Mukhida) 16-17 (all). The photographs on pages 4, 8-9, 12-15, 18-19 and 23-9 were taken by APM Photographic. The artwork on the cover and on pages 6-7 is by Jackie Harland. We would like to thank the staff and children at Somerhill Junior School, Hove, Sussex, for their kind assistance.

Index

Words in **bold** indicate subjects that are shown in pictures. 'g' indicates glossary entry.